Sprucing Up the Castle
with X-Blocks®

BY PATRICIA PEPE
with Andrea Macy & Arielle Pepe

Dedication

to my husband Alan
who is the King of my castle

Acknowledgements

I WANT TO THANK

Jesus Christ my Lord
and shepherd of my soul;
whose steadfast love and mercy
never ends

Andrea Macy - a true princess, whose friendship and encouragement is a blessing in my life,
My daughter and friend Arielle Pepe - her life is one of God's miracles of mine,
My son Barrett for his tender and loving spirit and amazing creativity
and my daughter Michelle for her love and thoughtfulness

Cheryl Phillips - God bless you! You are a treasure to me

The X-Blocks Testers Team for checking and testing the patterns -
I really appreciate all their effort – they saved me a lot of work and frustration!
Alice Courtney, Pat McFeron, Marisol Rodarte, Pat Laputz, Gwen Radabaugh,
Marielle Mansfield, Lisa Marmon, Sandra Engle, Patricia Kelley & Jan Livingstone

Cover and interior illustrations: Gina Croce - ginartist@yahoo.com -
I cannot thank you enough for your beautiful artwork

Photography: Cindy Franklin - www.cindyfranklinphotos.com
an amazing photographer and friend

The photographs in Sprucing Up the Castle were taken at two spectacular California venues, The Apple Farm Inn in
San Luis Obispo and the Eagle Castle Winery in Paso Robles. They welcomed us with open doors and provided a
magnificent backdrop for the projects. The next time you travel through the central coast of California,
include them in your itinerary and thank them for their support.

Apple Farm Inn - 2015 Monterey Street
San Luis Obispo, CA 93401
(805) 544-2040 • www.applefarm.com
A Boutique Hotel Collection Property

Eagle Castle Winery - 3090 Anderson Road
Paso Robles, CA 93446
(805)227-1428 • www.eaglecastlewinery.com

And last but certainly not least -
Michelle, Tara and Steve at Palmer Printing for their patience and for continuing my vision -
I really couldn't do without them; they are such a joy to work with and help make every project a dream come true!

ISBN: 978-09815172-1-6

Contents

4. Once Upon a Time

5. Let Your Castle Makeover Begin! What are X-Blocks?

6. Getting Started

7. Happily Ever Afters – Finishing Techniques (Borders, Layering & Basting, Binding)

Projects

ROYAL BEDCHAMBER

9. Royal Resort, *Bed Scarf/Toe Warmer with X-tra's Pillow Shams*

15. Lap of Luxury, *Lap or Bed Quilt*

THE GREAT HALL

22. King's Ransom, *Quilt or Wall Art with 2 X-tra's floor pillows or wall art*

CASTLE KITCHEN AND ROYAL DINING

30. Table Scraps, *Topper with Apron and Hot-Pot Holders*

42. Toast & Jam, *Tablerunner with matching Placemats*

47. Diamond in the Rough, *Tablerunner/wall hanging with matching placemats*

53. Vining and Dining, *Tablerunner or Bed/Sofa Scarf with matching wall hanging*

EXOTIC ACCENTS

60. Posy Patch Pillows and Wall Art

63. Hither and Thither, *Floor pillow*

66. X-Blox, *Decorative cubes or pillows*

70. Crowning Touch, *Valance*

Once upon a time...

in the magical land of X-Blocks, the Quilt Queen went a-strolling through the Pieceful Palace. Spring had sprung and Queen Patricia could feel X-citement in the air. X-Blocks Land was in full bloom. The meadows were covered in soft, snuggly crazy-quilts and patchwork pathways meandered through hillsides adorned with color... It seemed like only yesterday she had created the wonderful X-Blocks tool and shared it with everyone in the land. The young and the not-getting-any-younger, the faint-hearted and the adventurous had all exclaimed: "How quick! How simple! How very X-TRAORDINARY!"

But now, as the Queen gazed out over the pieced paradise, she realized that the castle itself was not so cheery, and in fact was beginning to look a bit drab and dreary. The Quilt Queen pondered as she wandered through the halls, "my castle is beginning to look positively down in the moat—the décor looks like it's right out of the Dark Ages. I've decided! I'll do it – by royal decree. I'll use X-Blocks to bring the beauty outside...inside to me!"

She rushed hither and thither all the day through murmuring to herself. "Hmm – now what shall I do?...Those hillsides blooming with posies – they just tickle my toesies! I'm sure the design will look very divine gracing the foot of my bed. And look!...I'll toss in some pillows for under my head..."

"...That lovely floral meadow will be just the thing to inspire a tablecover fit for a king. Of course a new apron and some hot-pot holders would make a queen's heart sing...the look of those vines climbing up the rock walls –...she paused, catching her breath...will be an X-quisite woven tapestry to hang in the Great Hall–..."

"It's a Royal Makeover," she declared, "and it's been so much fun, I must share my ideas with everyone!"

So come join Queen Patricia and start your new adventure in X-Blocks Land, where you can fix-up and freshen-up and spruce up your castle, too!

Of course, everyone in X-Blocks Land is still sewing and singing and living happily...oh, you know the rest...

Let Your Castle Makeover Begin!

Welcome to X-Blocks Land where dozens of X-citing new designs are awaiting you. To make sure this X-Blocks adventure has a happy ending and you avoid frustration, read the pattern instructions carefully before cutting and sewing. You'll get your very best results this way.

The Magic Rotary Cutter Wand will point out tips and tricks along the way to help you on your journey.

What are X-Blocks®?

....you might be wondering if you're new to X-Blocks Land. X-Blocks are square acrylic tools designed for rotary cutting and are available in several sizes:

LARGE X-BLOCKS:

The 7½", & 6½" X-Blocks tools will give you a finished block size of 7" and 6". These can be used for bed-sized quilts, lap quilts and larger wall hangings, tablerunners, etc.

SMALL X-BLOCKS:

Mini and Bellybutton X-Blocks are much smaller tools which can be used to make wall hangings, tablerunners, pillows, borders and so much more. The Mini is ¼-th the size of the Large X-Blocks so 4 Mini's = 1 Large block. There is one Mini for each of the Large X-Blocks: Mini-7.5 and Mini-6.5. These are sized 4" and 3½", the finished block sizes are ½" smaller.

The Bellybutton fits the center of the nine-patch made for the large X-Blocks. There is one Bellybutton for each of the large X-Blocks: Bellybutton-7.5 and Bellybutton-6.5. These are sized 3¾" and 3¼", the finished block sizes are ½" smaller.

ALL THOSE LINES!

Don't let all the dots and dashes frighten you – they simply provide more ways to create wonderful designs. There are three different styles of lines on each X-Blocks tool; a solid line, a dashed line and a dotted line. The solid line uses the same measurement for all the fabric strips and segments. The dashed and dotted lines use two separate measurements for the fabric strips and segments to create unique designs. Each X-Blocks pattern states which line to use, and uses only one style of line.

THE MAGIC OF X-BLOCKS®

X-Blocks start with easy to piece strips or blocks that are sewn together first. Place the X-Blocks tool on the strips or blocks, match the seams with the designated line (solid, dash, dotted) to the lines of the tool and trim along the edges with a rotary cutter. Voila! You've got X-Blocks! It's that easy!

By flipping the X-Blocks over you'll create mirror images, turn squares into diamonds and turn straight lines into zigzags!

After you have cut all of your blocks according to the pattern directions, you will have perfectly square, uniform sized blocks that make construction a breeze.

Best of all there is virtually no waste – transform the 'X-tra's into a fabulous project!

That's the magic of X-Blocks!

Getting Started

SEAM ALLOWANCE

For best results, a generous ¼" seam allowance should be used when sewing the blocks or strips together to create the unique X-Blocks designs. Before you start your project, it is helpful to test your seam allowance by sewing a sample strip set or block. Place the X-Blocks tool you are using on the strip set or block and check to make sure the seams line up with the lines of the tool. Adjust your needle position or seam allowance if necessary.

NO WASTE

As you can see by the illustrations, a triangle wedge is trimmed off the corners of the blocks. This seems like a lot of wasted fabric but in reality, you are simply cutting the pieces for your border or next project! With the X-Blocks tool and patterns, you can create amazing projects using those trimmed pieces. In fact they are so valuable the Queen has named them her little X-tra's – the X-tra project or X-tra border that is part of the X-Blocks fun. It's like finding buried treasure! It's a good idea to set these X-tra pieces aside so you have them ready for the border or your next project. A small zip-top baggie keeps them from running amok in the sewing room and saves you a lot of time.

Helpful Hints from the Queen

- Before using your X-Blocks tool, remove the protective backing. Placing non-slip disks or film on both sides of the tool will help prevent movement when cutting with the rotary cutter.

- Use the full width of the fabric (42"- 44") when cutting strips, unless individual pattern directions state otherwise.

- Stripe fabrics work exceptionally well for many X-Blocks designs, however it is a good idea to test a stripe to see how it works in your chosen design. Different designs will emerge depending on where the stripe is placed in the original block.

- Some designs require the X-Blocks to be flipped over before cutting. Double check the placement of the X-Blocks tool before cutting each time.

- A rotating mat is very helpful when cutting your blocks with the rotary cutter.

- When pressing use a light spray starch such as Mary Ellen's Best Press.

- Place the X-tra's (cut off pieces from blocks) into zip-top bags to keep them from running amok.

- Use a design wall if at all possible –this helps visualize your design and avoid mis-placement of blocks.

Happily Ever Afters

FINISHING TECHNIQUES

This section covers the necessary steps to finish your project. There are many other technique books available if you find that additional instruction or information is needed.

Borders

1. Cut the specified number of border strips for your project and sew them together end to end to make a continuous strip. Trim the seam to ¼" and press open.
2. Measure through the center of the quilt or other project from top to bottom and cut 2 strips this measurement. Sew the strips to the sides; press seams to the border.
3. Measure through the center of project from side to side, including the borders you just added. Cut two strips that measurement and sew to the top and bottom. Press seams to the border.

Layering & Basting

If you are planning to quilt your project it will need to be layered with the batting and backing and then basted together. Your backing and batting should be at least 2" – 3" larger than your quilt top on each side. For some of the projects in this book, you will need to cut and piece the backing fabric so it is large enough. Press seams open. There are many wide backing fabrics available which provide a seamless back and save you the time of cutting and piecing.

1. Spread out the backing, wrong side up on a smooth work surface. Tape or pin down the edges so that the backing is taut.
2. Gently center the batting and smooth it over the backing. Work out any wrinkles in the batting.
3. Place the pieced quilt or other project right side up on the batting, checking that backing seams and edges are straight with the top. Smooth it until it is flat.
4. Use safety pins to hold the layers in place.

Start pinning in the center and work your way out toward the edges, placing pins every 4" – 5".

BINDING

If you choose to bind your project, use 2" wide straight grain strips, cut across the width of the fabric.

1. Cut the specified number of strips for your project and sew them together, end-to-end using a diagonal seam, to make one continuous strip. Trim the seam to ¼" and press open.
2. Fold and press the binding in half lengthwise with wrong sides together.
3. Starting in the center of one side of the quilt or project, place binding strip on right side of pieced top, raw edges even; leaving a 10" tail.
4. Sew binding to top, mitering corners. Stop approximately 15" from where you started.
5. Remove from sewing machine and lay on a flat surface. Place the tail of the first binding end in place on edge of quilt top. Repeat with second tail. Make a crease in the second tail where it meets the end of the first tail. Measure 2" from the crease and cut the second tail straight across at that mark.
6. Open both tails and place right sides together at a right angle. Sew a diagonal seam, trim to ¼" and press open. Re-fold binding strip in half lengthwise and finish stitching to edge of top.

Fold binding over edge of pieced top, hiding seam and stitch securely in place.

Royal Bedchamber

Royal Resort
Bed Scarf /Toe Warmer with X-tra's Pillow Shams

Lap of LuXury
Lap or Bed Quilt

Royal Resort

'When I first open my eyes upon the morning meadows
and look out upon the beautiful world, I thank God I am alive'

- Ralph Waldo Emerson

The bed scarf
moves to the dresser
or table top.
Add instant charm
by using soft,
romantic colors.

The princess uses the
scarf and sham to dress up
her table and mantle.
For a clever decorating focal
point use the pillow sham
to top your mantle.

Scarf and sham made by Andrea Macy

Materials

Yardages are based on 42" - wide fabrics

Finished Size	7½" X-Blocks 76" x 22"	6½" X-Blocks 66" x 19"
Asst. green, brown, tan, aqua prints for blocks	2¾ yds total	2¼ yds total
Dark brown for sashing	½ yard	½ yard
Light sashing	¼ yard	¼ yard
Backing fabric	2 yards	1¾ yards
60° triangle ruler		

Cutting Chart

WOF = width of the fabric (approx. 42")

	7½" X-Blocks	6½" X-Blocks
Asst. green, brown, tan, aqua prints for blocks	A - (24) 2½" x WOF B - (12) 1⅝" x WOF	A - (24) 2¼" x WOF B - (12) 1⅜" x WOF
Dark brown for sashing	(12) 1¼" x WOF	(12) 1¼" x WOF
Light sashing	(6) 1¼" x WOF	(6) 1¼" x WOF
Backing	78" x 24"	68" x 21"

Royal Resort **Bed or Sofa Scarf**

Made with the 7½" or 6½" **X-Blocks®** tool
Measurements for the 6½" X-Blocks are in
parentheses

MAKING BLOCKS

Referring to diagram sew together in the
following order: 2 **A** strips, 2 **B** strips and 2 more
A strips to make a 6-strip-wide set. Repeat to
make 6 sets of 6 strips each. Press seams of
3 strip sets toward the center, press seams of
remaining 3 towards the outside edges.

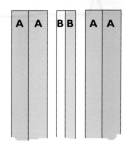

Cut 3 center-pressed strip-sets into 10 - 10¼"
(9¼") blocks.

Cut the remaining 3 strip-sets (w/seams pressed
to outside edges) into 10 - 10¼" (9¼") blocks.

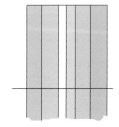 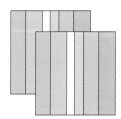

You should now have a total of 20 blocks; 10 w/
seams pressed to center and 10 w/seams pressed
to outside. Make sure to keep each set of blocks
in separate stacks according to the direction the
seams were pressed.

BASIC X-BLOCK

Place X-Blocks tool on a block from the first
set, (seams pressed toward center) making sure
the **right side of tool is facing up**, matching
dotted lines of tool to outside seams of center

strips (see diagram). Cut along edges of X-Blocks
with rotary cutter. Set aside the X-tra's (cut-off
wedges) to use for your pillow shams. Repeat to
make a total of 10 Basic X-Blocks.

↓ ↓

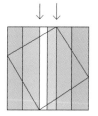

Basic X-Blocks

REVERSE X-BLOCK

Flip the X-Blocks tool over and place on a
block from the second set (seams pressed toward
outside edges), again matching dotted lines of
tool to outside seams of center strip. Cut around
edges of tool and set aside the X-tra's. Repeat to
make a total of 10 Reverse X-Blocks.

↓ ↓

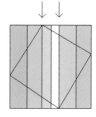

Reverse X-Blocks

Following Assembly Diagram sew blocks together
into 2 vertical rows of 10 blocks each, alternating
Basic and Reverse Blocks to create a zigzag
pattern, making sure each row starts with the
opposite block from the previous row. Press
seams in one direction. **Do not sew rows
together!**

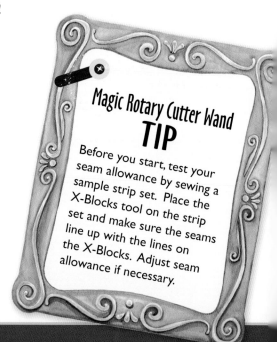

Magic Rotary Cutter Wand TIP

Before you start, test your seam allowance by sewing a sample strip set. Place the X-Blocks tool on the strip set and make sure the seams line up with the lines on the X-Blocks. Adjust seam allowance if necessary.

Royal Resort **Bed or Sofa Scarf**

SASHING STRIPS

Sew 6 dark sashing strips together end-to-end to create a continuous strip. (Be careful not to get tangled up). Repeat with remaining 5 dark sashing strips. Sew light sashing strips together end-to-end in the same manner.

Sew light sashing between dark sashing strips; press seams to the center. From this strip-set cut 3 - 70½" (60½") and 2 - 20½" (19½") pieces.

Sew long sashing pieces between block rows and to both long outside edges as shown in Assembly Diagram; press seams to sashing. Trim ends of sashing even with sides if necessary.

Add short sashing pieces to top and bottom edges of bed or sofa scarf and press toward the sashing strip.

FINISHING:

Layer lightweight batting or flannel, backing (right side up) and pieced scarf (right side facing down); pin edges in several places to secure. Stitch ¼" around outside edges, backstitching and leaving a 10-12" opening. Trim seam allowances at corners.

Turn right side out. Press and stitch opening closed. Topstitch the layers together in several places and along edges of sashing.

Place on the end of your bed or the back of your sofa, put your feet up, relax and take it easy!

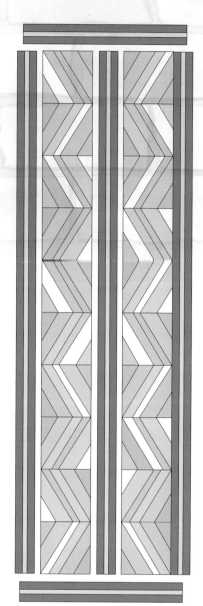

Assembly Diagram

Royal Resort X-tra's Pillow Shams

Made from X-tra's of blocks from bed or sofa scarf

ADDITIONAL MATERIALS

Yardages are based on 42" wide fabrics

FOR EACH PILLOW SHAM	7½" X-BLOCKS	6½" X-BLOCKS
Dark Brown for border and backing	¾ yd.	¾ yd.

CUTTING CHART

WOF = Width of Fabric (approx. 42")

CUT FOR EACH PILLOW SHAM	7½" X-BLOCKS	6½" X-BLOCKS
Dark Brown for border and backing	(2) 3½" x 11½" (2) 5½" x 28" (2) 21" x 15"	(2) 3½" x 9½" (2) 5" x 28" (2) 21" x 14"

Separate the X-tra's into 2 stacks: 1 with horizontal strips and 1 with vertical strips.

Sew 2 of the X-tra's (with vertical) together to create a triangle. Try to vary the colors opposite each other. It is helpful to pin this seam to prevent movement. Press seams open or to one side. Make 12 triangles from both the horizontal and vertical strip X-tra's. Trim the bottom edge of triangles; with a 60° ruler, trim all triangles to the same size, approx. 6" (5") high.

Sew 6 triangles together side by side alternating horizontal and vertical strip triangles. Sew an X-tra wedge to square ends of row as shown.

Repeat the above steps to make a second row, placing the horizontal and vertical triangles so they connect to the row above as shown in diagram.

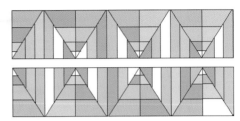

Add short border strips to sides; press to border. Sew long border strips to top and bottom of pillow front; press to border. Trim ends of border strips even at sides if necessary.

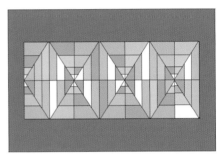

Hem one long edge of each pillow back with a ¼" seam. Place the two pillow back pieces, with the hems at the center, over the pillow front with right sides together and raw edges matching, overlapping one half over the other so that the measurement across the back is the same as the pillow front. Baste in place across overlap on top and bottom edges.

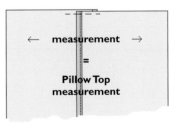

Sew around outside edges. Trim the corners, turn right side out through opening in back; press seams flat. Topstitch on pillow front through all layers along the border seam to create flange if desired. Insert pillow through opening in back.

Lap of Luxury

'Reflect upon your present blessings,
of which every man has many...'

- Charles Dickens

Vibrant color energizes this bedroom. Colors from the quilt reappear in accent pillows and accessories.

Floral fabrics in golden yellow and deep coral add warmth and comfort to this cozy quilt. The bright green accent adds a trellis effect in this lap throw.

Made by Lisa Marmon

Materials

Yardages are based on 42" - wide fabrics

Finished Size	7½" X-Blocks 70" x 83"	6½" X-Blocks 60" x 72"
Light background	3½ yds.	3¼ yds.
Asst. prints or solids	3¼ yds.	3 yds.
Green print	¾ yd.	⅔ yd.
Inner border	⅓ yd.	⅓ yd.
Outer border	1¼ yds.	1 yd.
Backing and binding fabric	6 yds.	5 yds.

Cutting Chart

WOF = width of the fabric (approx. 42")

	7½" X-Blocks	6½" X-Blocks
Light background	B1 - (12) 6½" x WOF B2 - (28) 4¼" x 10¼" B3 - (4) 4¼" x WOF B4 - (4) 6½" x 10¼"	B1 - (12) 5¾" x WOF B2 - (28) 3⅞" x 9⅛" B3 - (4) 3⅞" x WOF B4 - (4) 5¾" x 9⅛"
Asst. prints or solids	(24) 4¼" x WOF (3) 2¾" x 20"	(24) 3⅞" x WOF (3) 2⅜" x 18"
Green print	(4) 2¾" x WOF (2) 6½" x WOF	(4) 2⅜" x WOF (2) 5¾" x WOF
Inner Border	(7) 1½" x WOF	(6) 1½" x WOF
Outer Border	(8) 5" x WOF	(7) 4½" x WOF
Backing Binding	(2) WOF x 90" (8) 2" x WOF	(2) WOF x 68" (7) 2" x WOF

Lap of LuXury Bed or Lap quilt

Made with the 7½" or 6½" **X-Blocks®** tool
Measurements for the 6½" X-Blocks are in parentheses

Note: You can also make this quilt with all interior blocks. Make 32 additional interior blocks in place of the border and corner blocks.

MAKING THE BLOCKS
INTERIOR BLOCKS

Sew B1 strip to a wide color strip to make strip set; press seam to color strip. Repeat to make 13 sets; cut into 124 - 4¼" (3⅞") Segment A. Set aside 28 of these segments to use in your border blocks.

Sew narrow green strip between two different wide color strips to make strip set; press seams to green strip. Repeat to make 4 sets. Cut strip sets into 48 - 2¾" (2⅜") Segment B.

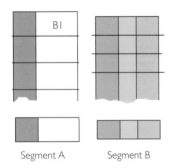

Sew a B segment between 2 A segments as shown to make block, placing the color patch in Segment A on opposite corners of block. Press seams with a light spray starch toward Segment B. Repeat to make 48 blocks.

Place the X-Blocks tool on top of a block, matching dotted lines of tool to the seams of the block.

Cut around the edges of the X-Blocks tool with a rotary cutter, setting aside the X-tra's*. Repeat with all 48 blocks.

Block A

After your blocks are cut, handle them gently as the edges are bias and will stretch if not careful. They are perfectly square and ready to sew into your quilt top.

BORDER BLOCKS

Sew wide green strip to wide color strip; press seam to green strip. Repeat. Cut into 28 - 2¾" (2⅜") Segment C.

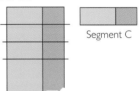

Segment C

Referring to diagram, sew Segment A (set aside from making interior blocks) and Segment C to B2 rectangle placing the color patches of the segments together. Press seams to the center strip; repeat to make 28 border blocks.

B2

Segment C   Segment A

Magic Rotary Cutter Wand
TIP

To save even more time & fabric, sew your strips together end-to-end before sewing into the strip sets. This will create a seam in some of your blocks, but it's almost impossible to see once it's quilted!

Lap of LuXury Bed or Lap quilt

Place the X-Blocks tool on top of block, matching dotted lines of tool to the seams of the block. Cut around the edges of the X-Blocks with a rotary cutter, setting aside the X-tra's*. Repeat with all 28 border blocks.

Border Block

CORNER BLOCKS

Sew a wide and a narrow color strip together; add B3 strip to narrow color strip. Press seams toward center. Cut into 4 - 4¼" (3⅞") Segment D.

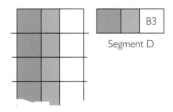

Segment D

Add B4 to pieced unit placing B3 patch in Segment D in upper right corner as shown. Make 4 blocks in this manner.

Segment D

Place X-Blocks tool on top of block matching dotted lines to the seams of the strip set. Cut around the edges of the X-Blocks with a rotary cutter.

Corner Block

QUILT TOP ASSEMBLY

TIP It might be easier to assemble the interior blocks first following assembly diagram, then add the corner and border blocks to the outer edges.

Referring to the Assembly Diagram and using a design wall if possible, arrange the blocks into 10 horizontal rows of 8 blocks each. Check the placement of corner and border blocks, rotating the blocks as needed to distribute the colors. Sew blocks into rows. Press the seam allowances in opposite directions from row to row. Sew the rows together, pressing the seam allowances in either direction or open when necessary to minimize bulk.

BORDERS

Sew border strips together end to end to make a continuous strip; press to one side. Add inner boreder to all sides of quilt following directions in Happily Ever Afters on page 7.

Add wide outer border strips to top and bottom of quilt in the same manner as for the inner border.

FINISHING THE QUILT

Layer, baste and quilt following directions in Happily Ever Afters on page 7.

*Since there is not a designated project for the X-tra's in this pattern, you could use them to make pillows or wallhangings as in the King's Ransom page 27-28

Lap of LuXury Bed or Lap quilt

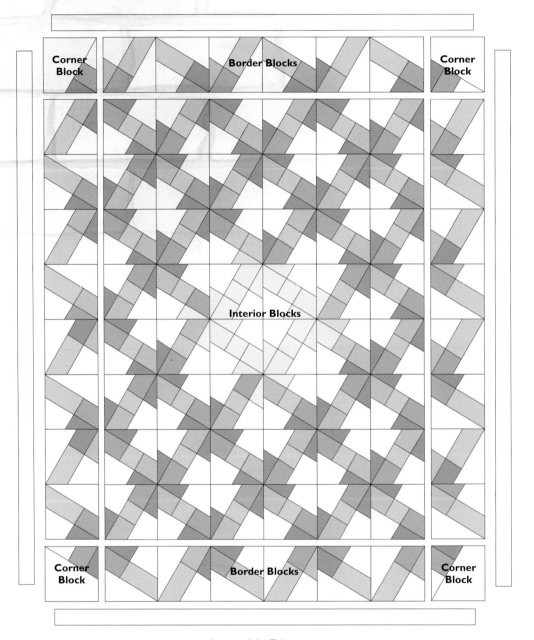

Assembly Diagram

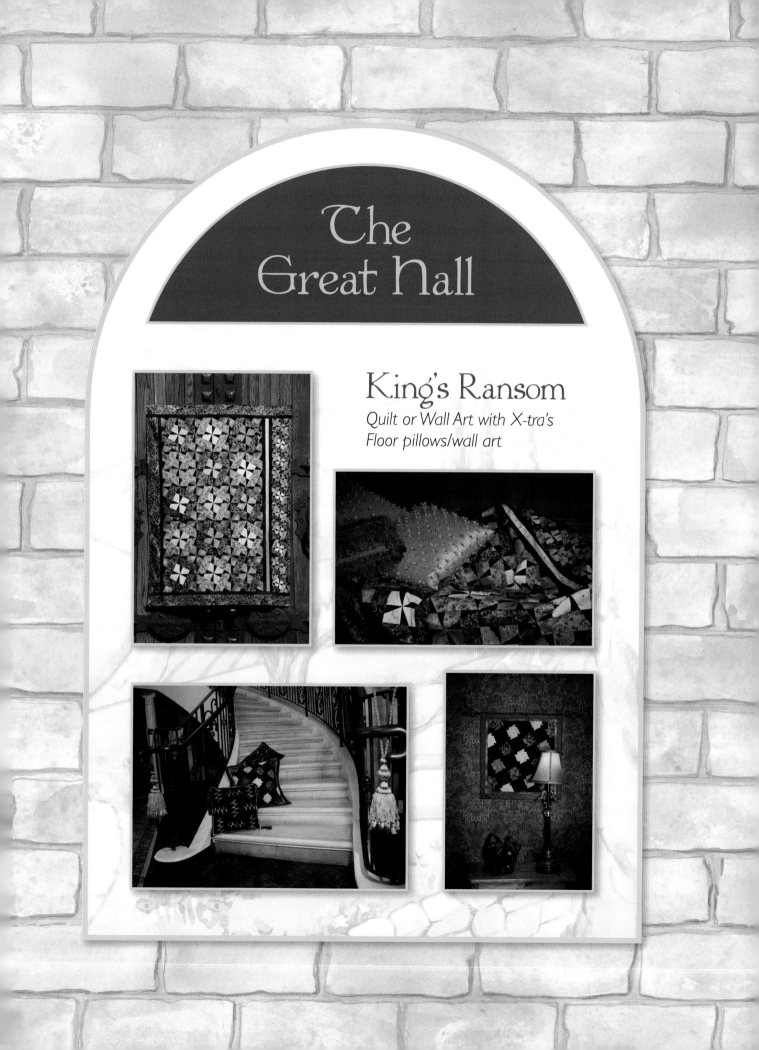

The Great Hall

King's Ransom

Quilt or Wall Art with X-tra's
Floor pillows/wall art

'For where your treasure is,
there your heart will be also'

- Matthew 6: 21

Turn up the bright and make this quilt in some of today's hottest decorating hues.

Good looks go to new heights when the quilt is used as an instant headboard.

Quilt made by Marielle Mansfield

Materials

Yardages are based on 42" - wide fabrics

Finished Quilt Size	7½" and Mini-7.5 X-Blocks 56" x 79"	6½" and Mini-6.5 X-Blocks 49" x 69"
Red background	3¼ yds.	2⅔ yds.
Gradated fabric	1 yd.	¾ yd.
Coral print	1¼ yd.	1 yd.
Light print	1¼ yds.	1 yd.
Dark print	1⅔ yds.	1⅓ yds.
Backing fabric	3¼ yds.	2¾ yds.

Cutting Chart

Cut all strips across the width of the fabric (approx. 42") = WOF

	7½" and Mini-7.5 X-Blocks	6½" and Mini 6.5 X-Blocks
Red background	24 strips 3¾" 8 strips 2⅛"	20 strips 3¼" 8 strips 1⅞"
Border	4 strips 1¼"	4 strips 1¼"
Gradated fabric	6 strips 3¾" 2 strips 2⅛"	5 strips 3¼" 2 strips 1⅞"
Border	2 strips 1¼"	2 strips 1¼"
Coral print	6 strips 3¾" 2 strips 2⅛"	5 strips 3¼" 2 strips 1⅞"
Border	6 strips 1¾"	6 strips 1¾"
Light print	8 strips 3¾" - Sub-cut into (32) rectangles 10¼" 4 strips 2⅛" - Sub-cut into (20) 5½" rectangles	8 strips 3¼" - Sub-cut into (32) rectangles 8¾" 4 strips 1⅞" - Sub-cut into (20) 4½" rectangles
Dark print	7 strips 3¾" - Sub-cut into (28) rectangles 10¼" 3 strips 2⅛" - Sub-cut into (20) 5½" rectangles	7 strips 3¼" - Sub-cut into (28) rectangles 8¾" 3 strips 1⅞" - Sub-cut into (20) 4½" rectangles
Outer Border	2 strips 1" 6 strips 3½"	2 strips 1" 6 strips 3¼"

King's Ransom   Quilt or Wall Art

Made with either the 7½" and Mini-7.5 or 6½" and Mini-6.5 coordinating Mini X-Blocks tools. This luXurious quilt or wall hanging was made with a gradated fabric in shades of pale yellow to light aqua – if you plan to use a gradated fabric try to find one with several different colors. To keep the design elements distinct, use fabrics with plenty of contrast.

Measurements for the 6½" and Mini-6.5 X-Blocks are in parentheses

MAKING THE BLOCKS

Sew a wide coral strip between two wide red background strips to make strip set A. Press seams to red strip. Make 6 (5) strip sets.

Sew a wide gradated strip between two wide red background strips to make strip set B. Press seams to red strip. Make 6 (5) strip sets.

Cut each strip set into 60 segments, 3¾" (3¼")

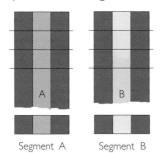

Segment A   Segment B

Sew a wide light print strip between one Segment A and one Segment B, visually aligning segment seams across strip. Press seams to light strip. Repeat to make 32 Block A.

Block A

In the same manner, sew a wide dark print strip between one Segment A and Segment B; press seams to dark strip. Repeat to make 28 Block B.

Block B

Place the X-Blocks tool on a Block A matching the solid lines of the tool to the seams of the block. Carefully cut along the edges of the X-Blocks tool with a rotary cutter. Set aside the X-tra's for your pillows/wallhanging. Cut all Block A and Block B in this manner.

Place blocks into separate stacks; Block A and Block B

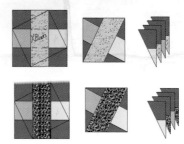

Remember – the edges of your cut blocks are bias. Handle them gently!

ASSEMBLING THE TOP

Sew 4 Block A together placing gradated patch to center, rotating each block 90° as shown to make a ring; press seams in either direction or open. Repeat with remaining blocks to make 8 Block A units and 7 Block B units.

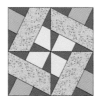

Block A Unit   Block B Unit

Magic Rotary Cutter Wand
TIP
Place the X-tra's (cut off pieces from blocks) into zip-top bags to keep them from running amok.

King's Ransom Quilt or Wall Art

Referring to Assembly Diagram, sew Block A and Block B units together into 5 rows of 3 blocks each, alternating A and B in each row. Press seams in either direction or open.

Sew narrow coral and wide outer border strips together; press to outer border strip. Measure length of quilt through center; cut a piece of border strip this measurement; set aside remainder. Sew the coral side to left side of quilt top; press seam to border.

Sew narrow gradated border strip between 2 red background border strips; press seams to red strips. Measure length of quilt as above cut border strip this measurement and sew this strip set to right side of quilt top; press seam to border strips.

MINI X-BLOCKS BORDER

Repeat the instructions for making Block A and Block B, using the narrow strips and cutting segments $2^{1/8}$" for Mini-7.5 and $1^{7/8}$" for Mini-6.5. Make 20 Mini Block A and 20 Mini Block B. Cut with Mini X-Blocks tool in the same manner as for the large blocks. Sew 2 of each Block A and Block B into unit as shown; press seams in either direction. Repeat to make 20 Block A & B units.

Sew AB units together as shown to make long strip, 10 blocks long. Sew 2 narrow print strips together end-to-end; measure length of AB-unit and cut to that measurement. Sew to one long edge; press seam to strip.

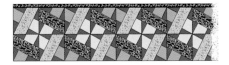

Sew Mini X-Blocks (AB-units) to the border strips on the right side of quilt top; press seam toward quilt.

Sew narrow coral and outer border strip together; press seam to outer border. Measure width of quilt as before; sew to top and bottom edges of quilt top.

FINISHING

Cut backing fabric and batting 3"-4" larger than quilt on all sides. Layer in this order: backing (right side facing down), batting, and pieced top (right side facing up); hand or pin baste; quilt as desired and finish with binding.

Assembly Diagram

King's Ransom X-tra's Pillows/Wallhanging #1

Made with X-tra's from quilt/wall art
(Measurements for X-tra's from 6½" X-Blocks tool in parentheses)

Sew the X-tra's with coral points and light print points together as shown, offsetting triangles and lining up the seams of the points. (Save the remaining X-tra's for pillow or wallhanging #2). Press seam in either direction. Repeat to make total of 36 rectangles. Trim all to $2^{1}/_{8}$" x 6½" ($1^{7}/_{8}$" x 6") rectangle.

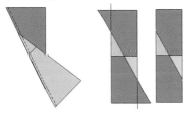

Sew 4 rectangles together placing the same color point on each side to make pieced unit. In the same manner sew remaining rectangles together into groups of four to make a total of 9 pieced units; press seams in either direction or open. Trim each unit to 6½" (6") square if necessary.

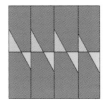

Sew 3 pieced units together to make a row, rotating each unit 90° so the points face in opposite directions.

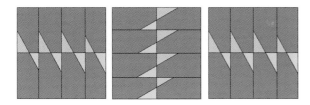

Repeat to make 2 more rows, having the points of each row face in opposite direction from the previous row. Press seams in either direction or open. Cut and sew a 1" wide strip of gradated fabric to all sides of pillow top. Add a 2" wide strip of red background fabric to all sides in the same manner.

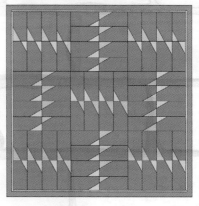

FOR PILLOW: Hem one long edge of each pillow back with a ¼" seam. Place the two pillow back pieces, with the hems at the center, over the pillow front with right sides together and raw edges matching, overlapping one half over the other so that the measurement across the back is the same as the pillow front. Baste in place across overlap on top and bottom edges.

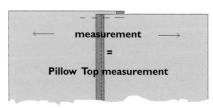

Place pillow back and front right sides together; sew around outside edges. Trim the corners, turn right side out through opening in back; press seams flat. Insert pillow form through opening in back.

FOR WALL HANGING: Layer on a flat surface in this order: batting, backing (right side facing up) and pieced wallhanging (right side facing down); pin in place. Beginning near the center of bottom row stitch around entire outer edge, ending stitching about 8-10" from beginning. Trim outside corners just to stitching line. Gently turn right side out; press and stitch opening closed. Quilt as desired to secure layers.

To make hanging sleeve, cut a strip of fabric 18" x 2½"; press and sew the side edges ¼" to the inside. With right sides together sew long edges with ¼" seam, backstitching at each end. Turn right side out. Hand stitch long edges of sleeve to the back at the top edge of wall hanging.

King's Ransom X-tra's Pillows/Wallhanging #2

Made with X-tra's from quilt/wall art (Measurements for X-tra's from 6½" X-Blocks tool in parentheses)

Sew the X-tra's with dark print and gradated points together into rectangles as shown. Press seams in either direction or open. Repeat with all dark-print and gradated point X-tra's. Trim rectangles to 2¾" x 5¾" (2½" x 5"). Make 42.

Cut 8 - 3½" (3") squares from both gradated and dark print fabrics. Sew a 3½" (3") gradated square to X-tra's rectangle as shown, stopping ½" from end of square. Press seam to pieced rectangle.

Add another X-tra rectangle to left side of unit with a full seam; press toward the pieced rectangle.

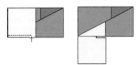

Continue adding X-tra's around the square until all 4 rectangles are sewn on and then finish the partial seam. Repeat steps to make a total of 9 X-tra's blocks. Trim blocks to 8" (7") square if necessary.

Using the same partial seam technique, sew pieced blocks to dark print squares as shown. Continue adding pieced blocks and dark print squares, filling in with additional pieced units. You will end up with uneven sides.

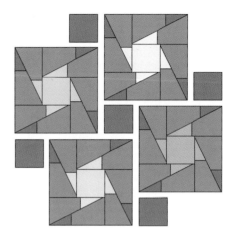

Trim evenly on all sides to make square. Finish following directions for pillow or wallhanging #1.

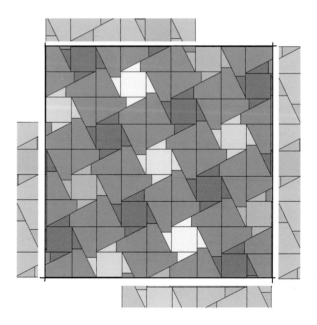

Castle Kitchen & Royal Dining

Table Scraps
Table topper or Picnic Throw with Apron & Hot-Pot Holders

Coast & Jam
Tablerunner with matching Placemats

Diamond in the Rough
Tablerunner or wallhanging with matching Placemats

Vining & Dining
Tablerunner or Bed/Sofa Scarf & wall art

'Taste and see
that the Lord is good'

- Psalm 34: 8

*An updated and
vibrant look for this
apron and hot-pad
set will chase the
hum-drum right out
of the kitchen!*

Quilt, Apron and
Hot Pot Holder made
by Sandra Engle

*Get the look of yesteryear
with a table cover made
with fabric right out
of the scrap bag.*

Materials

Yardages are based on 42" - wide fabrics

Finished Size	7½" X-Blocks 65" x 65"	6½" X-Blocks 58" x 58"
Green background	2⅔ yds.	2 yds.
Asst. 1940's reproduction prints	2 yds. total	1¾ yd. total
Yellow sashing	¾ yd.	⅔ yd.
Red fabric for cornerstones	¼ yd.	¼ yd.
Red rick-rack	6¼ yds.	5½ yds.
Optional Outer Border	1 yd.	¾ yd.
Backing	3 yds.	2½ yds.

Cutting Chart

WOF = width of the fabric (approx 42")

	7½" X-Blocks	6½" X-Blocks
Green background	23 strips 3¾"	20 strips 3¼"
Cut strips into 245 squares	3¾" x 3¾" (1 strip yields 11 squares)	3¼" x 3¼" (1 strip yields 12 squares)
Asst. 1940's reproduction prints	18 strips 3¾"	17 strips 3¼"
Cut strips into 196 squares	3¾" x 3¾" (1 strip yields 11 squares)	3¼" x 3¼" (1 strip yields 12 squares)
Yellow sashing	17 strips 1½"	14 strips 1½"
Cut strips into 84 rectangles	7½" x 1½" (1 strip yields 5 rectangles)	6½" x 1½" (1 strip yields 6 rectangles)
Red Cornerstones Cut strips into 36 squares	2 strips 1½" 1½" x 1½"	2 strips 1½" 1½" x 1½"
Optional Outer Border	6 strips 5 ½" x WOF	5 strips 5" x WOF

Cable Scraps **Table Topper**

Made with the 7½" or 6½" **X-Blocks**® tool
Measurements for the 6½" X-Blocks are in parentheses

If you prefer a plain border instead of the pieced X-tra's border use X-Press Alternate Piecing directions on page 35 when making your blocks.

MAKING THE BLOCKS

Sew together 4 of the same print squares and 5 background squares as shown to make a nine-patch block. Press seams to the background fabric. Repeat to make a total of 49 nine-patch blocks – *using a different print in each nine patch block.*

Press all blocks with light starch or starch alternative.

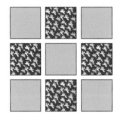

Place X-Blocks tool on a nine-patch block, matching the <u>solid</u> lines of the tool to the seams of the block. Cut along edges of X-Blocks tool with rotary cutter. Set aside the X-tra's (cut-off wedges) to use for your border. Cut all blocks in this manner.

<u>Handle blocks gently after cutting – the edges are bias and will stretch</u>

ASSEMBLY

Sew a sashing rectangle to the right side of 6 blocks; press seams to the sashing. To help prevent bias stretch, sew sashing strips to blocks with strip on top.

  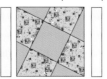

Referring to diagram, sew 6 sashed blocks together; press seams to sashing. Add an un-sashed block to the end to make a row. Repeat to make a total of 7 sashed rows. Set aside.

Sew a cornerstone to a sashing rectangle, press seam to sashing. Repeat to make a total of 36 sashing/cornerstone units.

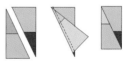

Sew 6 sashing/cornerstone units together end-to-end as shown; add a sashing strip to end. Press seams to sashing. Repeat 5 times to make a total of 6 sashing/cornerstone strips.

Sew block rows and sashing/cornerstone rows together into seven rows of 7 blocks each as shown in Assembly Diagram. Press seams toward sashing strips. *Note: There is no sashing on outside edges of topper.*

MAKING THE X-TRA'S BORDER

Sew the X-tra's together as shown to make wedge rectangles. Trim all rectangles to a same size, approximately 2¾" x 5¾" (2½" x 5"). Divide rectangles equally into 4 stacks.

Sew each stack of X'tra's rectangles together as shown to make 4 border strips.

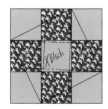

Table Scraps Table Topper

Cut a strip of background fabric the same width as the pieced border. Measure across center of topper from edge to edge. Cut 2 pieces from background fabric and sew to each end of X'tra's border strip to equal the measurement of top, sew to side of topper pressing seam in either direction. Repeat for remaining 3 sides of topper. Topstitch rick-rack over border seam if desired.

FINISHING

For a lighter weight table cover, place finished top and backing fabric right sides together and sew around all edges with ¼" seam allowance, leaving an opening of about 10" (piece backing fabric and cut to fit). Clip corners; turn right side out. Press edges and stitch opening closed. Topstitch lightly to keep layers together.

For a heavier weight table cover or lap quilt, cut backing fabric and batting 2"-3" larger than finished top. Layer and baste backing, batting and top. Quilt as desired and finish with binding.

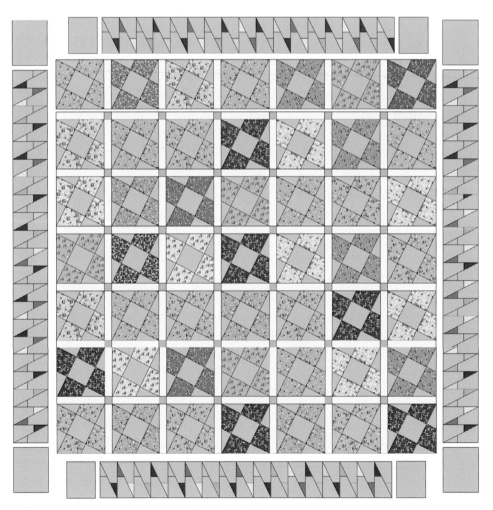

Assembly Diagram

Table Scraps Table Topper

X-PRESS ALTERNATE PIECING

Use the method below to make your blocks if you do not intend to make the pieced border from the X-tra's (cut-off pieces from blocks).

MATERIALS

	7½" X-BLOCKS 65" x 65"	6½" X-BLOCKS 58" x 58"
Green background	2 yds.	1¼ yds.
Asst. 1940's reproduction prints	2 yds. total	1¾ yds. total

CUTTING

	7½" X-BLOCKS 65" x 65"	6½" X-BLOCKS 58" x 58"
Green background	16 strips 3¾"	12 strips 3¼"
Cut strips into: 196 rectangles 49 squares	3¾" x 2¼" 3¾" x 3¾"	3¼" x 2" 3¼" x 3¼"
Asst. 1940's reproduction prints	18 strips 3¾"	17 strips 3¼"
Cut strips into: 196 squares	3¾" x 3¾"	3¼" x 3¼"

MAKING THE BLOCKS

Sew 4 of the same print squares and 5 background pieces together as shown to make a nine-patch block. Press seams to the background fabric. Repeat to make a total of 49 nine-patch blocks – using a different print in each nine patch block. Press all blocks with light starch or starch alternative.

Place X-Blocks tool on a nine-patch block, matching the solid lines of the tool to the seams of the block. Cut along edges of X-Blocks with rotary cutter. Cut all blocks in this manner.

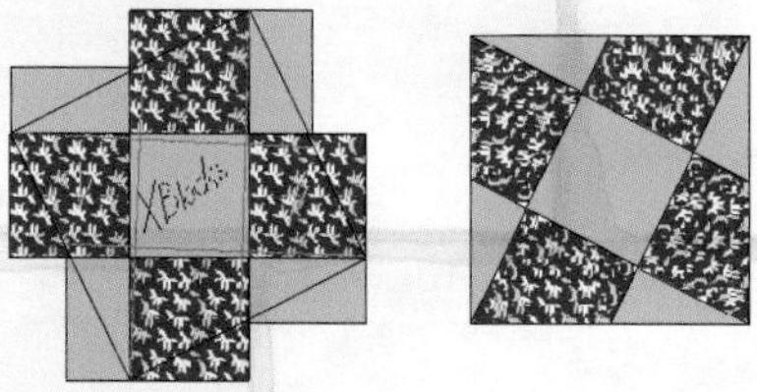

Handle blocks gently after cutting – the edges are bias and will stretch

After making blocks, continue assembly using the directions for table topper and substituting fabric in place of the X-tra's pieced border.

Table Scraps Apron

Made with the 7½" or 6½"' **X-Blocks®** tool
Measurements for 6½" X-Blocks are in
parentheses.

	7½" X-BLOCKS	**6½" X-BLOCKS**
Green background for blocks and apron front	(1) 24" × 32¼" (20) 3¾" × 3¾"	(1) 20" × 28¼" (20) 3¼" × 3¼"
Asst. 1940's reproduction prints	3¾" × 3¾" Cut 16 total – 4 from each print	3¼" × 3¼" Cut 16 total - 4 from each print
Sashing	(3) 1½" × 7½"	(3) 1½" × 6½"
Red for waistband	¼ yd.	¼ yd.
Rick-rack trim	2½ yds.	2¼ yds.

Following directions for nine-patch blocks for table topper, make 4 nine-patch blocks *using a different print in each block.*

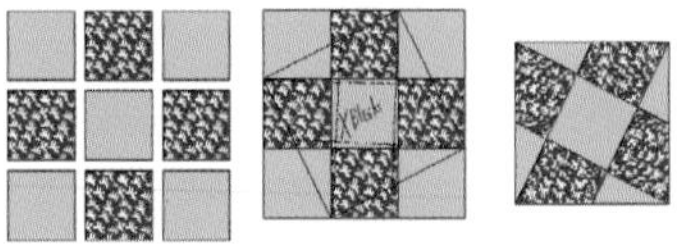

Sew sashing between the center blocks as shown. Press all blocks with light starch or starch alternative.

On **wrong** side of apron fabric, measure down from top edge 8", (7" if using 6½" X-Blocks); mark lightly with chalk or press a crease. Place one long edge of sashed nine-patch blocks right side down on marked line, ¼" in from outside edges. Sew across blocks with 1/4'' seam. Flip blocks up at seam; press.

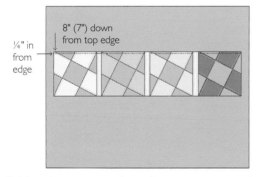

Fold and press top edge of apron over top of blocks. Sew rick-rack trim through all layers along top edge covering raw edge of apron fabric.

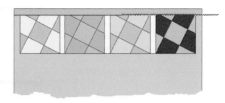

Fold blocks up to right side of apron fabric to create pocket. Baste along sides. Sew along sashing from top of pocket to bottom edge through all layers, backstitching at both ends. Press side edges of apron fabric to front ¼", covering edge of outside blocks. Sew rick-rack trim along edges covering raw edge of apron fabric. Baste or make pleats along top edge to desired width or fullness.

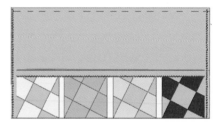

Press under ¼" and top stitch down long edges of ties. Fold in half lengthwise at one end and stitch across the diagonal as shown, backstitching. Trim off outside corner ¼" from seam. Turn end points right side out; press.

Press ¼" to inside both sides of waistband. Press up ¼" on one long edge; press waistband in half lengthwise, right sides together. Center right side of un-pressed edge of waistband to gathered edge of apron and stitch with 3/8" seam. Press waistband up and over seam. Insert end of ties between waistband (gather slightly if necessary); pin and stitch across edge, securing ties. Topstitch along bottom folded edges of waistband from end to end making sure to catch the back folded edge.

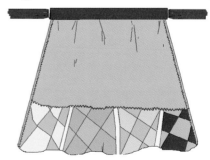

Table Scraps Hot-Pot Holder and Trivet

Made with X-tra's from Table Scraps Topper or Apron

Referring to diagram, sew X-tra's together to make rectangle; press seams in either direction. Repeat to make 4 rectangles for each hot-pot holder, 8 for each trivet. Trim all to same size, approx. 2¾" x 5¾" (2½" x 5½").

Sew X-tra's rectangles in a counterclockwise direction around center square in the order shown. Make a partial seam when sewing the first rectangle; add remaining rectangles with full seam; press toward rectangles.

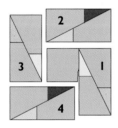 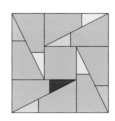

Make hanging loop by sewing long edges of 1½" x 6" rectangle right sides together. Turn right side out. Fold in half to make a loop. Baste loop to one corner of block with raw ends facing out.

Layer block and backing right sides together; place two squares of batting the size of block on top of the layered square. Sew around all edges leaving a 2"-3" opening. Trim corners slightly, turn right side out. Stitch opening closed and topstitch to secure layers.

For trivet make 2 blocks following directions for hot-pot holder using 8 X-tra's rectangles. Sew blocks together; press seams to one side. Finish the same as hot pot holder.

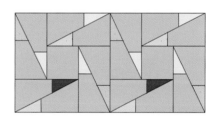

Bring majestic beauty into your home with a lap quilt that beckons with richness and comfort.

King's Ransom Pg. 22

Create a peaceful spot to sit back and let your cares vanish.

Quilt made by Gwen Radabaugh
Lap of Luxury Pg. 15

Put your personality in the spotlight with a table topper that adds warmth and charm to your home.

Topper made by Pat Laputz
Vining & Dining Pg. 53

You can create a festive mood just about anywhere in your castle with this colorful valance.

Crowning Touch Pg. 70

A lavish dose of deep color, rich folds of fabric and a generous sprinkling of accessories creates an elegantly appointed room.
King's Ransom Pg. 22

Weave romance into any room with a tablerunner made in rich floral tones.
Tablerunner made by Marisol Rodarte
Toast & Jam Pg. 42

Add depth and dimension to your scheme with a design that will satisy your passion for pattern.
Wallhanging made by
Pat Laputz
Vining & Dining Pg. 53

Bright fabrics and festive patterns create a space that sparkles with life.
Posy Patch pillow (center) by
Debby Baird, pg. 60,
King's Ransom pillow (left) by
Marielle Mansfield, pg. 22

Dramatize the entrance with a wallhanging that warms the walls of your castle (or moat).
Royal Resort Pg. 9

Color Forecast: Rich & Sophisticated - Deep colors in this simple design create a look of elegance and style.

King's Ransom X-tra's pillows Pg. 22

Energetic colors and a dazzling array of designs will revitalize any area of your home.

Table Scraps (on table) made by Sandra Engle, Pg. 30
Wall hangings (left) made by Pat Laputz, Vining & Dining Pg. 53, (center, right) made by Patricia Kelley (pattern not available)

Bring serenity and calm to your space with a simple yet sophisticated color scheme.

Tablerunner made by Andrea Macy Royal Resort Pg. 9

Settle down with some lemonade and cookies with a table dressed in cozy colors.

Tablerunner made by Pat McFeron Toast & Jam Pg. 38

Any seating is made more cozy with cushions or throw pillows.

King's Ransom X-tra's pillows Pg. 22

Decorative accents add a touch of whimsy and add interest to your decor. Go ahead and have a little fun!

X-Blox Pg. 66

Spice up a neutral space with a feeling of sunshine and flowers; mimic the bright colors of a garden bursting into bloom.

Lap of Luxury Pg. 15

Discover decorating drama and excitement with a vibrant wallhanging used as a focal point.

Wallhanging made by Alice Courtney
Diamond in the Rough Pg. 47

Toast & Jam

Tablerunner made by Marisol Rodarte

*'It is the sweet, simple things of life which
are the real ones after all'*

- Laura Ingalls Wilder

Quick and clever way to add instant sparkle to your room - Add a new spin by framing the placemat for X-tra special art.

Sweeten your indoor retreat with this charming tablerunner.

Materials

Yardages are based on 42" - wide fabrics

Finished Quilt Size	7½" X-Blocks 36½" x 22½"	6½" X-Blocks 32" x 20"
Y Yellow	½ yd.	½ yd.
DG Dark green	¼ yd.	¼ yd.
LG Light Green	¼ yd.	¼ yd.
C Coral	¼ yd.	¼ yd.
Border	¼ yd.	¼ yd.
Backing fabric	1 yd.	1 yd.

Cutting Chart

WOF = width of the fabric (approx. 42")

	7½" X-Blocks	6½" X-Blocks
Y Yellow	4 strips 3¾" x WOF From 2 strips cut: (8) rectangles - 3¾" x 7" (4) 3¾" squares	4 strips 3¼" x WOF From 2 strips cut: (8) rectangles - 3¼" x 6" (4) 3¼" squares
DG Dark green	2 strips 3¾" x WOF From strips cut: (16) 3¾" squares	2 strips 3¼" x WOF From strips cut: (16) 3¼" squares
LG Light Green	2 strips 3¾" x WOF From strips cut: (12) 3¾" squares	2 strips 3¼" x WOF From strips cut: (12) 3¼" squares
C Coral	1 strip 3¾" x WOF 3 strips 1¼" x WOF From 1¼" strips cut: (2) 16" lengths (2) 28½" lengths	1 strip 3¼" x WOF 2 strips 1¼" x WOF From 1¼" strips cut: (2) 14" lengths (2) 24½" lengths
Border	(2) 3½" x 30" (2) 3½" x 22"	(2) 3¼" x 26" (2) 3¼" x 20"
Backing fabric	38½" x 24½"	34" x 22"

Coast & Jam Tablerunner

Made with the 7½" or 6½" **X-Blocks®** tool

Measurements for the 6½" X-Blocks are in parentheses.

MAKING THE BLOCKS

Sew long coral strip between 2 yellow strips; press seams to coral strip.

Cut strip set into 8 - 3¾" (3¼") segments

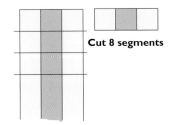

Cut 8 segments

Sew one segment together with yellow, dark green and light green patches as shown in diagram to make Block A; press seams in direction of arrows. Repeat to make 4 Block A.

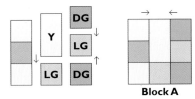

Block A

Referring to diagram, sew 2 more segments together with yellow, dark green and light green patches to make Block B; press seams in direction of arrows. Repeat to make 2 Block B.

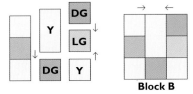

Block B

Sew last 2 segments together with yellow, dark green and light green patches as indicated to make Block C (Note direction change of Y rectangle in block.); press seams in direction of arrows. Repeat to make 2 Block C.

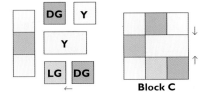

Block C

CUTTING THE BLOCKS

Place X-Blocks tool on a Block A, matching solid lines of tool to seams of block; cut around edges of tool with rotary cutter. Repeat with all Block A, B and C in the same manner.

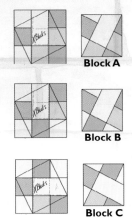

Block A

Block B

Block C

Sew blocks together into four rows of two blocks each, carefully following Assembly Diagram and rotating blocks as needed. It is helpful to place the blocks on a design wall or other area so you can step back to view them. Press seams in either direction or open.

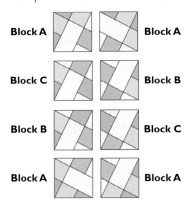

Block A		Block A
Block C		Block B
Block B		Block C
Block A		Block A

Sew narrow coral border to all sides. Sew long border strips to sides; press to border. Sew border strips to top and bottom in the same manner.

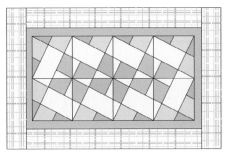

Coast & Jam Tablerunner

FINISHING

For a light weight tablerunner, place backing and pieced top right sides together. Sew around all edges with ¼" seam, leaving an opening of about 8-10". For a heavier weight tablerunner, place a layer of flannel or batting to wrong side of backing and finish as above. Trim corners; turn right side out. Press edges and stitch opening closed. Topstitch lightly along center design, around dark and light green outer patches and along border seams to keep layers together.

Coast & Jam Placemats

MATERIALS

Yardages are based on 42" wide fabrics

FOR EACH PLACEMAT	7½" X-BLOCKS	6½" X-BLOCKS
Y – Yellow background	¼ yd.	¼ yd.
DG – Dark green	¼ yd.	¼ yd.
LG – Light Green	⅛ yd.	⅛ yd.
C – Coral	⅛ yd.	⅛ yd.
Border	2" × WOF	2" × WOF
Backing	1 fat quarter or 18" × 22"	1 fat quarter or 18" × 22"

CUTTING CHART

WOF = Width of Fabric (approx. 42")

CUT FOR EACH PLACEMAT	7½" X-BLOCKS	6½" X-BLOCKS
Y – Yellow background	(4) 3¾" × 7" (8) 3¾" × 3¾"	(4) 3¼" × 6" (8) 3¼" × 3¼"
DG – Dark green	(8) 3¾" × 3¾" (2) 3" × 14½"	(8) 3¼" × 3¼" (2) 2¾" × 12½"
LG – Light Green	(8) 3¾" × 3¾"	(8) 3¼" × 3¼"
C – Coral	(4) 3¾" × 3¾"	(4) 3¼" × 3¼"
Inner border	(2) 1½" × 14½"	(2) 1½" × 12½"
Backing	21" × 14½"	18½" × 12½"

Sew patches together following diagram to create block; press seams in direction of arrows. Repeat to make a total of 4 blocks for each placemat.

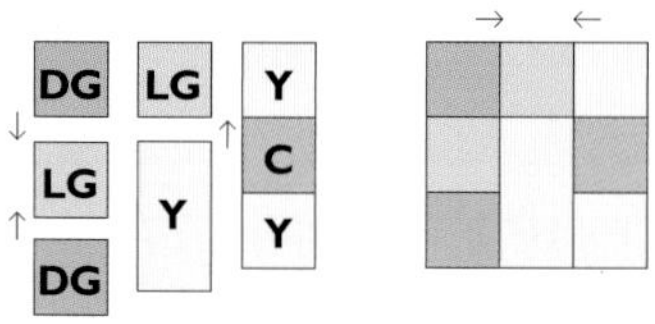

Place X-Blocks tool on a block matching solid lines of tool to seams of block. Cut around edge of tool with rotary cutter. Repeat with remaining 3 blocks.

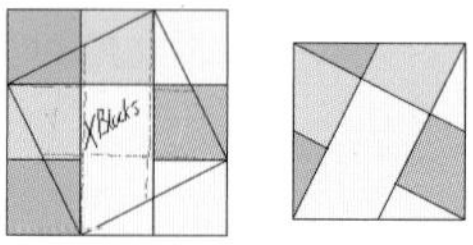

Referring to diagram sew blocks together rotating each block 90°, placing the coral patch toward the center. Press seams in either direction or open.

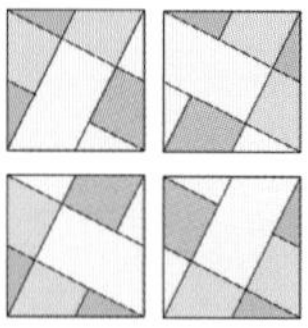

Sew narrow plaid border strip to two sides of placemat. Press seams to strip. Sew dark green strips to plaid border; press seams to the green strips. Finish in the same manner as for the tablerunner.

Magic Rotary Cutter Wand TIP

Before you start, test your seam allowance by sewing a sample strip set. Place the X-Blocks tool on the strip set and make sure the seams line up with the lines on the X-Blocks. Adjust seam allowance if necessary.

Diamond in the Rough

'Dreams are illustrations...from the book
your soul is writing about you'

- Marsha Norman

The new look begins at the door with a wall hanging that adds a touch of your personality.

Wallhanging in bright jewel tones hangs from a banister to create a dramatic entry.

Runner made by Alice Courtney

Materials

Yardages are based on 42" - wide fabrics

Fabric Finished Size	7½" X-Blocks 47" x 22"	6½" X-Blocks 41" x 16"
Gradated Background	⅓ yd.	⅓ yd.
Assorted Prints	⅔ yd. total	½ yd. total
Blacke	½ yd.	⅓ yd.
Coral & Aqua accent	¼ yd. each	¼ yd. each
Backing	¾ yd. if pieced, or 1½ yds.	⅝ yd. if pieced, or 1¼ yds.

Cutting Chart

Cut all strips across the width of the fabric (WOF) - 42" - 44"

Fabric	7½" X-Blocks	6½" X-Blocks
Gradated Background	3 strips 3¾"	3 strips 3¼"
Assorted Prints	5 strips 3¾" sub-cut into (15) -10¼" rectangles	5 strips 3¼" sub-cut into (15) - 8¾" rectangles
Black Solid	1 strip 3¾" sub-cut into (3) - 10¼" rectangles 3 strips 2½" x WOF	1 strip 3¼" sub-cut strip into (3) - 8¾" rectangles 3 strips 2" x WOF
Coral accent	3 strips 1" (3) 3¾" x 10¼" rectangles	3 strips 1" (3) 3¼" x 8¾" rectangles
Aqua accent	(3) 3¾" x 10¼" rectangles	(3) 3¼" x 8¾" rectangles

Diamond in the Rough Tablerunner/Wallhanging

Made with the 6½" or 7½" **X-Blocks®** tool
(The 7½" tool makes a very large finished size – it might also be used as a sofa or bed scarf)

Measurements for 6½" X-Blocks are in parentheses

This looks great made with a variety of ethnic prints, animal prints or groups of similar type designs. Accent fabrics create sparkle and add interest.

MAKING THE BLOCKS

Sew 4 (5) print rectangles onto one side of long gradated strip, as shown in diagram. Cut strip between rectangles.

Add a print or accent rectangle to opposite side of gradated strip to make block. Press seams to center strip. Repeat to make a total of 6 blocks.

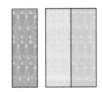

Sew remaining print and accent rectangles to gradated strips as above, pressing seams to the outside, to make 6 more blocks. Place blocks into separate stacks according to direction of pressed seams.

BASIC X-BLOCKS

With blocks from first set (seams pressed to center) place X-Blocks tool on a block matching solid lines of tool to the seams of the block. Cut around edges of the X-Blocks with rotary cutter. Repeat with all blocks from first set.

Basic X-Blocks

REVERSE X-BLOCKS

Flip the X-Blocks tool over (the printed words on the tool will appear backward). Place the flipped X-Blocks tool on a block from second set, matching solid lines to seams. Cut around the edges with a rotary cutter. Repeat with all blocks from second set.

Reverse X-Blocks

ASSEMBLY

Referring to the assembly diagram, sew blocks into 2 vertical rows alternating basic and reverse blocks and placing batik and color accents in a pleasing arrangement. Press seams in opposite directions. Sew rows together matching seams and ends. Press seams in either direction or open.

Cut and sew narrow coral border strip to all sides; press to strip. Cut and sew black border strip to all sides of tablerunner in the same manner; press seams to border.

Optional Outer Print Border:

Sew random lengths of print strips together, press seams to one side. Cut and sew 2 pieces to the long sides of tablerunner. Cut 2 more pieces and sew to top and bottom in the same manner. Press to print strip.

FINISHING

For a light weight tablerunner, place backing and pieced top right sides together.

Sew around all edges with ¼" seam, leaving an opening of about 8-10". Clip corners; turn right side out. Press edges and stitch opening closed. Topstitch lightly to keep layers together. For a heavier weight tablerunner, place a layer of flannel or batting to wrong side of backing and finish as above.

Diamond in the Rough Tablerunner/Wallhanging

Optional Pieced border

Assembly Diagram

Diamond in the Rough Placemats

Made with either the Mini-7.5 or Mini-6.5 X-Blocks®

Measurements for Mini-6.5 X-Blocks are in parentheses where indicated.

MATERIALS

Yardages are based on 42" wide fabrics

FINISHED SIZE	MINI-7.5 X-BLOCKS 17" X 23"	MINI-6.5 X-BLOCKS 14" X 21"
Gradated Background	1/3 yd.	1/3 yd.
Prints	2/3 yd. total	1/2 yd. total
Black	5/8 yd.	1/2 yd.
Coral & Aqua accent	1/4 yd.	1/4 yd.
Backing	1/2 yd.	1/2 yd.

CUTTING CHART

WOF = Width of Fabric (approx. 42")

	MINI-7.5 X-BLOCKS	MINI-6.5 X-BLOCKS
Gradated Background	(8) $2^{1}/_{8}$" × $5^{1}/_{2}$"	(8) $1^{7}/_{8}$" × $4^{5}/_{8}$"
Assorted Prints	(12) $2^{1}/_{8}$" × $5^{1}/_{2}$"	(12) $1^{7}/_{8}$" × $4^{5}/_{8}$"
Solid Black	1 strip $1^{1}/_{4}$" × WOF (2) $2^{1}/_{8}$" × $5^{1}/_{2}$" (1) $16^{1}/_{2}$" × $16^{1}/_{2}$"	1 strip $1^{1}/_{4}$" × WOF (2) $1^{7}/_{8}$" × $4^{5}/_{8}$" (2) $14^{1}/_{2}$" × $14^{1}/_{2}$"
Coral & Aqua accent	(2) $2^{1}/_{8}$" × $5^{1}/_{2}$" (1) ¾" × WOF (1) ¾" × $16^{1}/_{2}$"	(2) $1^{7}/_{8}$" × $4^{1}/_{8}$" (1) ¾" × WOF (1) ¾" × $14^{1}/_{2}$"

MAKING THE BLOCKS

Referring to illustrations for tablerunner sew a gradated rectangle between 2 different print rectangles to make block. Repeat with all rectangles placing gradated fabric in center each time to make a total of 12 blocks. Press seams of 6 blocks to center, seams of remaining 6 blocks to the outside and place into separate stacks according to direction of pressed seams.

Place Mini-X-Blocks tool on a block from first stack, matching the solid lines of X-Blocks tool to the seams. Cut around the edges of the tool with a rotary cutter to make Basic X-Block. Repeat with all blocks in first stack.

Flip the X-Blocks tool over (the printed words on the tool will appear backward). Place the flipped X-Blocks tool on a block from second stack matching seams to solid lines as before. Cut around the edges of the tool with a rotary cutter to make Reverse X-Block. Repeat with remaining blocks in second stack.

Diamond in the Rough Placemats

ASSEMBLY

Referring to diagram, sew blocks together
to make two diamonds, alternating Basic and
Reverse X-Blocks and placing fabrics in a pleasing
arrangement. Press seams open.

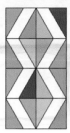

Sew narrow coral strip to black strip; press seam
to black strip. From this cut 2 pieces 7½" (6½")
and 1 piece 16½" (14½"). Sew the coral side of
shorter pieces to top and bottom of diamond
panel; press seam to coral.

Sew 16½" (14½") piece to left side; press seam
to coral strip.

Sew coral strip to right side of diamond panel;
sew square black panel to coral strip; press to
panel.

FINISHING

Layer batting, backing (right side facing up) and
placemat (right side facing down); pin in place.
Sew around all sides leaving a 6"-8" opening.
Trim corners. Turn right side out; press and
stitch opening closed. Topstitch layers together
along edges of coral strips and outline diamond
pattern. Stitch additional design in black rectangle
if desired.

Vining & Dining

GARDEN

Wallhanging made by Andrea Macy

'Life is a glorious banquet, a limitless
and delicious buffet'

- Maya Angelou

This design allows you the opportunity to take a formal approach or be whimsical - wherever your creative notions and design ideas take you.

Materials

Yardages are based on 42" - wide fabrics

Finished Size	7½" X-Blocks bed or sofa scarf 62" x 20"	6½" X-Blocks bed or sofa scarf 54" x 18"	Mini-7.5 Mini-6.5 X-Blocks tablerunner or wallhanging 33" x 12" 29" x 11"	Bellybutton-7.5 Bellybutton-6.5 X-Blocks tablerunner or wallhanging 31" x 11½" 27" x 9½"
B - Black Background	1 yd.	1 yd.	½ yd.	½ yd.
O - Orange (vertical weave)	½ yd.	½ yd.	¼ yd.	¼ yd.
R - Red (horizontal weave)	¼ yd.	¼ yd.	¼ yd.	¼ yd.
Backing fabric	1¾ yds.	1½ yds.	1 yd.	1 yd.

Cutting Chart

WOF = width of the fabric (approx. 42")

	7½" X-Blocks	6½" X-Blocks	Mini-7.5	Mini-6.5	Bellybutton-7.5	Bellybutton-6.5
B - Black Background Border	(8) 3¾" x WOF (3) 1½" x WOF	(8) 3¼" x WOF (3) 1½" x WOF	(2) 2⅛" x WOF (4) 2⅛" x 22" (2) 1" x 28½"	(2) 1⅞" x WOF (4) 1⅞" x 22" (2) 1" x 24½"	(2) 2" x WOF (4) 2" x 22" (2) 1" x 26½"	(2) 1¾" x WOF (4) 1¾" x 22" (2) 1" x 22½"
O - Orange (vertical weave)	(4) 3¾" x WOF	(4) 3¼" x WOF	(1) 2⅛" x WOF (2) 2⅛" x 22"	(1) 1⅞" x WOF (2) 1⅞" x 22"	(1) 2" x WOF (2) 2" x 22"	(1) 1¾" x WOF (2) 1¾" x 22"
R - Red (horizontal weave)	(2) 3¾" x WOF	(2) 3¼" x WOF	(2) 2⅛ x 22"	(2) 1⅞" x 22"	(2) 2" x 22"	(2) 1¾" x 22"

Segment Cutting Chart

	7½" X-Blocks	6½" X-Blocks	Mini-7.5 X-Blocks	Mini-6.5 X-Blocks	Bellybutton- 7.5 X-Blocks	Bellybutton- 6.5 X-Blocks
Cut segments	3¾"	3¼"	2"	1"	2"	1"

Vining and Dining Tablerunner or Bed Scarf/Sofa Scarf

You will be making 4 different blocks for this pattern. They are labeled **A**, **B**, **C**, & **D**. Place a sticky note or scrap of paper on stacks of blocks to avoid mixing them.

NOTE: Use the smaller X-Blocks tools to make the tablerunner and wallhanging and the larger tools (7½" & 6½" for the bed/sofa scarf.

MAKING THE BLOCKS

Blocks A & B

Sew an orange strip between 2 black background strips lengthwise to make strip-set.

If using the 6½" or 7½" X-Blocks:

Sew **2** strip-sets as above; press seams of one strip-set to the center and one to the outside.

If using Mini or Bellybutton X-Blocks:

Sew 1 strip-set as above; press seams toward the center on half of the length, press to the outside on the other half.

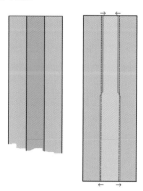

CUTTING THE BLOCKS

Place X-Blocks tool **right side up** on the strip set with seams pressed toward center, matching solid lines of tool to seams of block. Cut around edges of tool. Continue down the strip set cutting a total of 4 Basic X-Blocks. Label these **Block A**.

 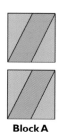

Block A

Flip the X-Blocks tool over and place on the strip set with seams pressed toward the outside, again matching solid lines of tool to seams of block. Cut around edges of tool. Continue cutting a total of 4 Reverse blocks in this manner making sure the X-Blocks tool is still flipped over. Label these **Block B**.

 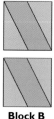

Block B

Blocks C & D

Sew an orange strip between 2 background strips lengthwise to make strip-set; press seams to outside. Sew a red strip between 2 background strips to make strip set; press seams to center. Cut strip-sets into 8 segments each referring to Segment Cutting Chart for measurement.

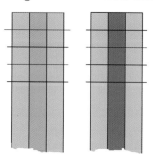

Orange Segment   Red Segment

Magic Rotary Cutter Wand TIP

It is helpful to use a light spray starch when pressing. Once your blocks are cut you will want to handle them gently since the edges are bias and will stretch if not treated carefully. If the blocks do get slightly stretched, they can be re-cut using the X-Blocks tool as before.

Sew 4 orange segments to red strip (horizontal weave) as shown, matching raw edges and butting each segment up against the edge of previous segment. Cut red strip between segments; press seam toward strip.

Add remaining 4 orange segments to opposite side of red strip making sure segment seams align visually across strip. Press seam to strip.

With X-Blocks tool **right side up place** on a block matching solid lines to seams; cut around edges of tool. Repeat to make a total of 4 Block **C**.

Block C

Sew red segments to orange strip (vertical weave) in the same manner as for Block C.

Add remaining 4 red segments to opposite side of orange strip making sure segment seams align visually across strip. Press seam to strip.

Flip the X-Blocks tool over and place on block, matching seams to solid lines; cut around edges of tool. Repeat to make a total of 4 Block D.

Block D

ASSEMBLY

Following Assembly Diagram, arrange Blocks A,B,C, & D into 2 columns of 8 blocks each, making sure the same colors connect to the block before it. Sew together; press seams in either direction or open.

Sew inner border strips to all sides of tablerunner; press to border.

Add outer border strips to all sides in the same manner.

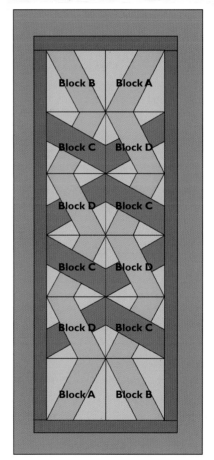

Assembly Diagram

FINISHING

Layer pieced top and backing right sides together. If desired, place lightweight batting or flannel behind backing. Sew around edges leaving 4"-5" opening. Trim corners; turn right side out, press and stitch opening closed. Top stitch through all layers following outline of design on fabric if desired and stitching along the weave strips.

Vining and Dining Wallhanging

Make a stunning wall hanging to complete the look by adding some decorative fabric or a pre-printed panel! This is a great way to use that large print you love but don't know what to do with.

First, choose which X-Blocks tool to use. Find the height of your fabric on the chart below for the suggested size X-Blocks tool.

To use the complete X-Blocks woven design, follow these recommendations.

Suggested use

Fabric Height:	X-Blocks tool:
up to 25"	Bellybutton-6.5
24" to 27"	Mini-6.5
26" to 29"	Bellybutton-7.5
28" to 35"	Mini-7.5

There is some crossover on the fabric size for the different tools. It is a good idea to make a test block to check the scale of the fabric/panel to the size X-Blocks tool used.

If a different size fabric/panel is used you can eliminate Blocks A and B at the top and bottom of pieced unit to fit (see Fig. 2)

Referring to the illustrations for the tablerunner, construct pieced unit in the same manner using the Mini or Bellybutton X-Blocks tools.

Measure height of decorative fabric/panel; compare to measurement of pieced unit. If necessary add back-ground strips to the fabric/panel or pieced unit at the top and bottom so both are equal measurement (see Fig 1 and Fig. 2).

Cut and sew border strips to long sides of pieced unit; press to border. Sew the pieced unit to right side of decorative fabric/panel; press seam to panel.

FINISHING

Finish in the same manner as the tablerunner. Add a hanging sleeve to back. To make hanging sleeve, press and sew the side edges of sleeve strip ¼" to the inside. With right sides together sew long edges with ¼" seam, backstitching at each end. Turn right side out. Hand stitch long sides of sleeve to the back at the top edge of wall hanging.

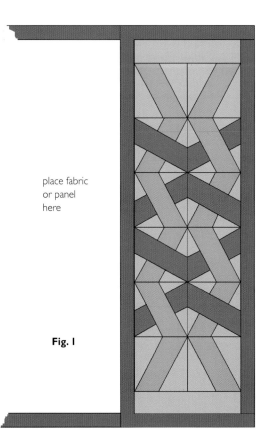

place fabric or panel here

Fig. 1

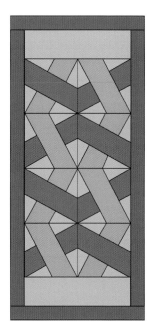

Fig. 2

eXotic Accents

Posy Patch
Pillows and Wall Art

Nither & Thither
Floor pillow

X-Blox
Decorative cubes or pillows

Crowning Touch
Valance

*'Friendship is the choicest flower that
grows in nature's garden'*

- Marcia Marshall

Materials

Yardages are based on 42" - wide fabrics

Fabric needed for each pillow	7½" X-Blocks	6½" X-Blocks	Mini-7.5 X-Blocks	Mini-6.5 X-Blocks	Bellybutton-7.5 X-Blocks	Bellybutton-6.5 X-Blocks
Background	⅓ yd.	⅓ yd.	⅛ yd.	⅛ yd.	⅛ yd.	⅛ yd.
Color for Posy	⅛ yd.	⅛ yd.	5" square	5" square	5" square	5" square
Green	⅛ yd.	⅛ yd.	5" square	5" square	5" square	5" square
Backing fabric	15" square	13" square	9" square	8" square	9" square	8" square
Decorative trim	1¾ yd.	1½ yd.	1 yd.	1 yd.	1 yd.	1 yd.
Pillow stuffing	—	—	—	—	—	—

Cutting Chart

WOF = width of the fabric (approx. 42")

Cut for each pillow	7½" X-Blocks 14" pillow	6½" X-Blocks 12" pillow	Mini-7.5 X-Blocks 6½" × 6½"	Mini-6.5 X-Blocks 6" × 6"	Bellybutton-7.5 X-Blocks 6¼" × 6¼"	Bellybutton-6.5 X-Blocks 5½" × 5½"
Background	(4) 7" × 7" (12) 3¾" × 3¾"	(4) 6" × 6" (12) 3¼" × 3¼"	(4) 3¾" × 3¾" (12) 2⅛" × 2⅛"	(4) 3¼" × 3¼" (12) 1⅞" × 1⅞"	(4) 3½" × 3½" (12) 2" × 2"	(4) 3" × 3" (12) 1¾" × 1¾"
Color for Posy	(4) 3¾" × 3¾"	(4) 3¼" × 3¼"	(4) 2⅛" × 2⅛"	(4) 1⅞" × 1⅞"	(4) 2" × 2"	(4) 1¾" × 1¾"
Green	(4) 3¾" × 3¾"	(4) 3¼" × 3¼"	(4) 2⅛" × 2⅛"	(4) 1⅞" × 1⅞"	(4) 2" × 2"	(4) 1¾" × 1¾"
Backing fabric	14½" × 14½"	12½" × 12½"	7½" × 7½"	6½" × 6½"	7" × 7"	6" × 6"

Posy Patch Pillows and Wallhanging

PILLOW

MAKING THE BLOCKS

For each pillow you will make 4 blocks: Sew patches together as shown to make block, pressing seams in direction of arrows. Repeat to make a total of 4 blocks.

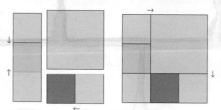

With X-Blocks tool right side up, place on a block matching solid lines of tool to seams. Cut around edges of tool with rotary cutter; set aside X-tra's. Repeat with remaining 3 blocks.

Sew four blocks together as shown, rotating each block 90° and placing the pink flower patches toward the center.

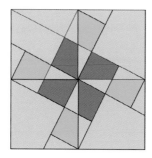

Pin trim (rick-rack, pom-poms, etc) along outside edges of pillow top making sure trim is facing to the inside; machine baste in place. Place backing and pillow top right sides together. Pin securely; stitch around all edges leaving 4-5" opening for turning. Trim corners and turn right side out.

Stuff pillow lightly and sew opening closed. With a long needle, sew decorative button through center of posy on pillow top, securing stitching with small button on back.

WALL HANGING

For the wall hanging you will make 3 different posies using the colors in reverse placement as in the pillow, i.e. black for posy, color for background. For each posy panel you will make 4 blocks in the same manner as for the pillow:

Sew patches together as shown to make block, pressing seams in direction of arrows. Repeat to make a total of 4 blocks.

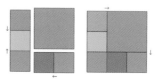

With X-Blocks tool right side up, place on a block matching solid lines of tool to seams. Cut around edges of tool with rotary cutter; set aside X-tra's. Repeat with remaining 3 blocks.

Sew four blocks together as shown, rotating each block 90° and placing the pink flower patches toward the center.

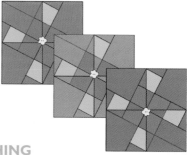

FINISHING

With posy and backing right sides together sew around edges leaving an opening for turning. Trim corners, turn right side out and sew opening closed. Topstitch around posy motif and in green leaf areas. Attach hanging sleeve.

For Instant Art you can mount a posy block to pre-stretched canvases. Add 3" borders to sides of posy block. Center block on a canvas that is 2-3" smaller than your unfinished block. Fold border fabric over sides of canvas and staple to frame. Fold corners in first, secure with staple then fold in sides and staple.

Nither & Thither

'Not all those that wander are lost'
- J.R.R.Tolkien

Hither and Chither Floor Pillow

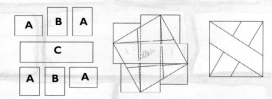

BASIC X-BLOCKS CHART
X-Blocks tool used right side up

Each block has 4 background rectangles (A),
2 color rectangles (B) and 1 color strip (C)

	A (4) background rectangles	**B** (2) color rectangles	**C** (1) color strip
ROW 1	Block 1 Block 3	Orange Pink	Yellow Yellow
ROW 2	Block 2 Block 4	Red Purple	Lt. Green Lt. Green
ROW 3	Block 1 Block 3	Orange Pink	Green Green
ROW 4	Block 2 Block 4	Red Purple	Blue Green Blue Green

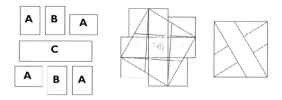

REVERSE BLOCKS CHART
X-Blocks tool flipped over

Each block has 4 background rectangles (A),
2 color rectangles (B) and 1 color strip (C)

	A (4) background rectangles	**B** (2) color rectangles	**C** (1) color strip
ROW 1	Block 2 Block 4	Yellow Yellow	Red Purple
ROW 2	Block 1 Block 3	Lt. Green Lt. Green	Orange Pink
ROW 3	Block 2 Block 4	Green Green	Red Purple
ROW 4	Block 1 Block 3	BlueGreen BlueGreen	Orange Pink

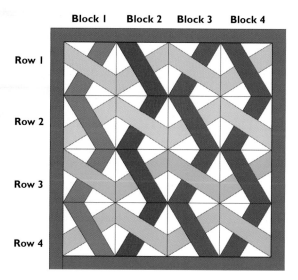

	Block 1	Block 2	Block 3	Block 4
Row 1				
Row 2				
Row 3				
Row 4				

MATERIALS

	Background Cut 64 total	**'B' Rectangles** Cut 4 each color	**'C' Strips** Cut 2 each color
7½" X-Blocks	¾ yd.	⅛ each color	⅛ each color
6½" X-Blocks	¾ yd.	⅛ each color	⅛ each color
Mini-7.5	¼ yd.	⅛ each color	⅛ each color
Mini-6.5	¼ yd.	⅛ each color	⅛ each color
Bellybutton-7.5	¼ yd.	⅛ each color	⅛ each color
Bellybutton-6.5	¼ yd.	⅛ each color	⅛ each color

CUTTING CHART

	'A' Rectangles Background Cut 64 total	**'B' Rectangles** Cut 4 each color	**'C' Strips** Cut 2 each color
7½" X-Blocks	3¼" × 4"	3¼" × 4"	3¼" × 10¼"
6½" X-Blocks	2¾" × 3½"	2¾" × 3½"	2¾" × 9⅛"
Mini-7.5	1¾" × 2⅜"	1¾" × 2⅜"	1¾" × 5½"
Mini-6.5	1⅝" × 2⅛"	1⅝" × 2⅛"	1⅝" × 4⅞"
Bellybutton-7.5	1¾" × 2¼"	1¾" × 2¼"	1¾" × 5¼"
Bellybutton-6.5	1½" × 2"	1½" × 2"	1½" × 4½"

hither and Chither Floor Pillow

MAKING THE BLOCKS

All blocks are made of rectangles and strips– there are no set in seams or triangles to sew. Make each block individually in order, referring to Assembly Diagram and Block Chart for fabric placement and whether it is a Basic or Reverse X-Blocks (see below). Each block consists of four background rectangles **(A)**, two of the same color rectangles **(B)**, and one color strip **(C)**. *Note: The blocks will have irregular sides – this is intentional. The patches for Reverse X-Blocks are placed opposite of those for Basic X-Blocks.*

BASIC X-BLOCKS

The diagram below shows construction for all Basic X-Blocks. These are made using the X-Blocks tool right side up (words appear right side).

Block 1, Row 1: Sew the orange rectangle (B) between two background (A) rectangles; press seams to the background. Repeat. Sew the yellow strip (C) between the two pieced units making sure the seams of the pieced units align visually across the strip as shown; press seams to the strip.

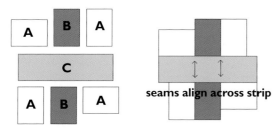

seams align across strip

With the X-Blocks tool **right side up**, place on block matching dashed lines of tool to seams of block. Cut around edges of tool with rotary cutter.

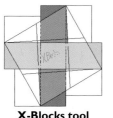

X-Blocks tool right side up

Basic X-Blocks
Block 1, Row 1

All blocks in the Basic X-Blocks Chart are made in this manner. Continue sewing each block together in order, following the chart for correct combination of fabrics.

REVERSE X-BLOCKS

The diagram below shows construction for all Reverse X-Blocks. These are made using the X-Blocks tool **flipped over** (words appear backward). *Note: The patches for reverse X-Blocks are placed opposite of those for Basic X-Blocks.*

Block 2, Row 1: Sew the yellow rectangle (B) between two background (A) rectangles; press seams to background. Repeat. Sew the red strip (C) between the two pieced units making sure the seams of the pieced units align visually across the strip as shown; press seams to the strip.

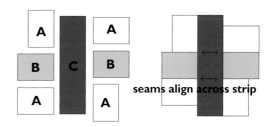

seams align across strip

Flip the X-Blocks tool over (words appear backward) and place on block matching dashed lines of tool to seams of block. Cut around edges with rotary cutter.

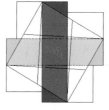
X-Blocks tool flipped over

Reverse X-Blocks
Block 2, Row 1

All blocks in the Reverse X-Blocks Chart are made in this manner.

Continue sewing each block together in order, following the chart for correct combination of fabrics.

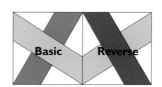
Basic   Reverse

'Thoughts lead on to purposes, purposes go forth to actions, actions form habits, habits decide character, and character fixes our destiny'

- anonymous

Create X-citing
decorative accents
with this quick
and easy project.

Combine a
variety of rich colors,
special prints and
textures for playful
sophistication
and style.

Materials

Yardages are based on 42" - wide fabrics

Fabric needed for each cube	7½" X-Blocks	6½" X-Blocks	Mini-7.5 X-Blocks	Mini-6.5 X-Blocks	Bellybutton- 7.5 X-Blocks	Bellybutton- 6.5 X-Blocks
Finished cube size	7"	6"	3½"	3"	3¼"	2¾"
Background	⅓ yd.	⅓ yd.	¼ yd.	¼ yd.	¼ yd.	¼ yd.
6 different color prints	8" square each print	7" square each print	5" square each print	5" square each print	5" square each print	5" square each print

Cutting Chart

WOF = width of the fabric (approx. 42")

Cut for each cube	7½" X-Blocks	6½" X-Blocks	Mini-7.5 X-Blocks	Mini-6.5 X-Blocks	Bellybutton- 7.5 X-Blocks	Bellybutton- 6.5 X-Blocks
Background Cut 30 squares	3¾" × 3¾"	3¼" × 3¼"	2⅛" × 2⅛"	1⅞" × 1⅞"	2" × 2"	1¾" × 1¾"
6 different color prints Cut 4 squares from each print (24 total)	3¾" × 3¾"	3¼" × 3¼"	2⅛" × 2⅛"	1⅞" × 1⅞"	2" × 2"	1¾" × 1¾"

X-Blox

The X-Blox cube is made from 6 X-Blocks. The instructions below use a standard nine-patch X-Blocks design however other X-Blocks designs can be used. All blocks must be made with the same size X-Blocks tool.

MAKING THE BLOCKS

Sew 4 print squares and 5 background squares together as shown to make a nine-patch block. Press seams to the print fabric. Repeat to make a total of 6 nine-patch blocks – using a different print in each nine patch block if desired. Press all blocks with light starch or starch alternative.

Place X-Blocks tool on a nine-patch block matching solid lines of the tool to seams of the block. Cut along edges of X-Blocks with rotary cutter. Repeat with all 6 blocks.

On wrong side of each block make a mark in each corner ¼" from the edge. Referring to diagram, sew 4 blocks in a row, starting and ending seams at marks, backstitching at both points on all seams. Press seams in either direction.

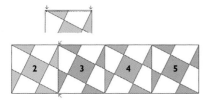

Sew Block 1 to the top of Block 2; sew Block 6 to the bottom of Block 5, again starting seam ¼" from ends and backstitching. Press seams in either direction. Topstitch a scant ¼" around unsewn edges of Blocks 1-5; use topstitching line to press the edges to the inside.

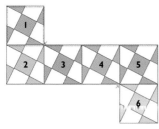

Fold unit in half right sides together and sew Block 5 to Block 2 along raw edges from point A to B, ¼" from ends as shown in diagram. The center blocks will form a tube.

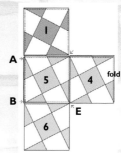

Open unit into a tube and fold up Block 6 to form bottom of cube. Sew and backstitch sides of Block 6 to corresponding side of Blocks 4, 3 and 2, using a ¼" seam

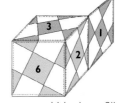

If using a foam or wood block to fill cube, fold Block 1 down to form top and sew to Blocks 3 and 5 about 1½", stitching right below top-stitching line, backstitching and leaving remaining seams open for turning.

If filling cube with stuffing, fold Block 1 down to form top and sew to Blocks 3, 4 and 5 leaving approx. 3" open for turning and stuffing.

Gently turn X-Blox right side out. Insert foam or wood block cut to fit or stuff lightly. Hand stitch opening.

Crowning Touch

'As the waves follow the sea, so may
God's blessings follow thee'
- unsigned

Enhance the view from any window when you dress it up with a two toned valance…or create softness to a doorway and add instant personality.'

Valance made by Sandra Engle

Materials

Yardages are based on 42" - wide fabrics

	7½" X-Blocks	6½" X-Blocks	Mini-7.5 Mini-6.5 X-Blocks	Bellybutton-7.5 Bellybutton-6.5 X-Blocks
Gold diamonds	⅓ yd.	⅓ yd.	¼ yd.	¼ yd.
Green diamonds & hanging sleeve	⅔ yd.	⅔ yd.	¼ yd.	¼ yd.
Lining	1 yd.	1 yd.	⅓ yd.	⅓ yd.

Cutting Chart

WOF = width of the fabric (approx. 42")

	7½" X-Blocks	6½" X-Blocks	Mini-7.5 X-Blocks	Mini-6.5 X-Blocks	Bellybutton-7.5 X-Blocks	Bellybutton-6.5 X-Blocks
Gold diamonds	(2) $4\frac{5}{8}$" × WOF	(2) $4\frac{1}{4}$" × WOF	(1) 3" × WOF	(1) $2\frac{1}{2}$" × WOF	(1) $2\frac{5}{8}$" × WOF	(1) $2\frac{3}{8}$" × WOF
Green diamonds & hanging sleeve	(2) $4\frac{5}{8}$" × WOF (2) 6" × WOF	(2) $4\frac{1}{4}$" × WOF (2) 6" × WOF	(1) 3" × WOF (1) 5" × WOF	(1) $2\frac{1}{2}$" × WOF (1) 5" × WOF	(1) $2\frac{5}{8}$" × WOF (1) 5" × WOF	(1) $2\frac{3}{8}$" × WOF (1) 5" × WOF
Lining	(2) 15" × WOF	(2) 14" × WOF	(1) 9" × WOF	(1) 8" × WOF	(1) 9" × WOF	(1) 8" × WOF

Crowning Touch Valance

The large X-Blocks tools (7½" & 6½") make great valances, mantle scarves etc., while the smaller X-Blocks (Mini's and Bellybutton's) can be used to decorate items such as the edge of a quilt, garment or wallhangings, etc. Use the Cutting Chart to determine the width of strips for the size X-Blocks tool you are using. The pattern is written for a valance made with two strips of each color. You can make it longer with additional strips.

TOP HALF OF DIAMOND
MAKE BASIC RECTANGLES

Sew the two color strips together lengthwise; press seam to right side.

Place X-Blocks tool **right side up** covering the right strip as shown, matching the dotted line on tool to the seam. *Note: the X-Blocks tool will hang off the strip set on left side.* Cut around edges of tool on top and right side of strip set; cut along bottom edge stopping at seam.

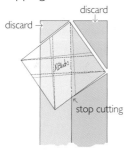

Move the X-Blocks over so that the left strip is now covered; match cut edges and dotted line on tool to seam. Cut remaining edge on left strip to make half-diamond rectangle. Continue cutting rectangles by moving the X-Blocks down the strips and cutting as before. Set aside the drop-off pieces to use for the bottom half of your diamond. These are your Basic rectangles.

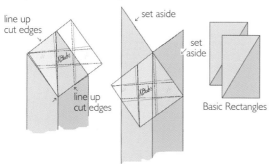

MAKE REVERSE RECTANGLES

Sew strips together in the same manner as for Basic rectangles but press lengthwise seam to left side.

Flip the X-Blocks tool over and place on left strip as shown (the tool will hang off the strip set on *right side*). Cut around tool in the same manner as previously. Move tool so the right strip is now covered; cut remaining edge. These are your Reverse rectangles.

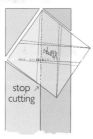

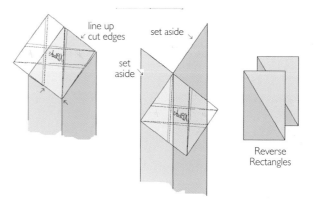

Sew the gold fabric side of a Basic and Reverse rectangle together as shown to make top half of diamond; press seams to right side. Repeat with all Basic and Reverse rectangles.

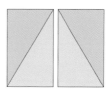

Crowning Touch Valance

BOTTOM HALF OF DIAMOND
MAKE BASIC TRIANGLES

The bottom half of the diamond is made with the triangle drop off pieces you set aside.

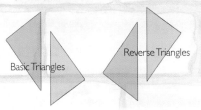

Basic Triangles

Reverse Triangles

Sew gold Basic and Reverse triangles together to make bottom half of diamond; press seams to left side. Repeat with all gold triangles.

ASSEMBLY

Sew top and bottom diamond halves together as shown; press seams in either direction. Sew the top rectangles together side by side to make continuous piece.

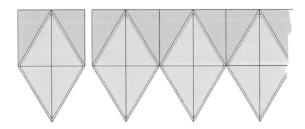

FINISHING

Layer backing and pieced diamond valance right sides together; sew around bottom pointed edges and up sides, leaving top edge open.
Clip inside corners and trim diamond points; turn right side out; press. Baste top edge closed.

Topstitch ½" from outside edges of diamonds hanging strips together end to end; press seam to either side. Press side edges to the inside and stitch down. Fold up one long edge of hanging strip ¼" and press. Sew un-folded edge of hanging strip to lining side on top edge of valance through all layers, backstitching at each end.

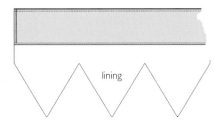

lining

Bring pressed/folded edge of hanging strip toward the front and place it over the stitching line; pin in place and topstitch along folded edge and ¼" from top edge through all layers, backstitching at both ends.

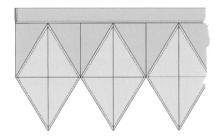

OPTIONAL DOUBLE DIAMOND

Sew the unused half of the drop off triangles together to make half diamond. Place together side by side overlapping about ½"; baste along edge where the triangles overlap.

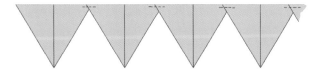

Layer backing and pieced half diamonds right sides together; pin in place and sew around bottom pointed edges and up sides, leaving top edge open. Clip inside corners and trim diamond points; turn right side out; press. Baste top edge closed. Position the half-diamonds behind diamond valance so the half diamonds show between the full diamonds. Hand stitch in place to secure.

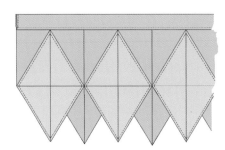

About the Authors

Arielle Pepe
Known as Princess Ari around the castle, she is Patricia Pepe's daughter, and works alongside 'Queen Mother' adding her creativity and knowledge to the business. She is earning her marketing/business degree; is intrigued by color, design and the magic of X-Blocks and hopes you enjoy this book as much as she does!

Patricia Pepe
Also known as the Quilt Queen, lives in her own little castle on top of a hill where she creates new adventures for X-Blocks Land without ever running out of ideas. She is a wife and mom, quilter, designer and inventor of the X-Blocks rotary cutting tool.

Andrea Macy
Enamored by the X-Blocks and X-citing possibilities, began as Patricia's quilt student and became a good friend. She loves her family, teaches quilting, and thanks God for each and every day. Especially for quilting days.

Additional X-Blocks Products

Once Upon a Time in X-Blocks Land book, X-Blocks tools and many other patterns available at your local quilt shop or from Quilt Queen Designs at www.quiltqueendesigns.com • www.x-blocks.com

Soli Deo Gloria